There Is a Field

Barbara Conrad

FUTURECYCLE PRESS

www.futurecycle.org

Cover photo by Artem Saranin; author photo by Katy Cobb;
cover and interior book design by Diane Kistner;
Philosopher text and titling

Library of Congress Control Number: 2018943989

Published by FutureCycle Press
Athens, Georgia, USA

ISBN 978-1-942371-54-0

for Esther

Contents

I

II

I

But this is not the story of a life.
It is the story of lives,
knit together, overlapping in succession,
rising again from grave after grave.

from *Rising*
Wendell Berry

In the Mingle of Gods

That summer I wandered Greece, I dared
my daughters to be safe, all three of us lifting from earth

the same week, one to London and Liverpool,
the other toting a backpack and boyfriend

through Europe. I prayed, *be safe, be safe,* as I paced
the Plaka, stumbled up steps to Athena's throne,

worked my breath, *in for one, hold for four, ahhh.*
Three points of light, split thin by vapor trails.

How could a mother suffer such turbulence?
                    *
A dream one night placed a lighted globe in my hands,
a primary school model, metal strip holding

the hemispheres taut, until it caught fire, melting oceans
and land masses into pulpy goulash, singeing my faith.

Gods were everywhere—voiceless now—lips, noses,
sex shattered by an ancient shift in creed.

Apollo, Dionysus, mere shadows. Even the oracle
in Delphi, when summoned, was as hushed

as the purple phlox in this field of old stones.
                    *
From my hotel bed in the small town, window sprung
for air, I woke to a keening in the night. It had to be

a mother, had to be for her child. Bent in black,
holding the broken body as family gathered

for the ritual procession through village streets.
What could I say that the gods did not.

That the earth would still hold her up, solid, spinning,
willing to keep making

its tedious orbit around the sun.

A Mother Dreams of Snow

Her boots are glass and lapis
lined in fur.

She hikes along an old mule path
from somewhere.

Drifts are high as the top
of her boots.

She turns into the woods, leaving
a moon and all its consistencies behind.

Under a black oak
she spots two small mounds in the snow,

frozen bunnies barely born.
She lifts and zips them into her jacket,

warms them on her breast until
they wiggle.

Warm breath on her skin.
And then, just then, an old farm house.

She enters to rummage for warmer gloves
and a box for the bunnies.

At the kitchen table, her two young daughters
are waiting for supper.

One asks where she's been,
why she hasn't fed them.

She startles—
she had thought her daughters were grown,

the older one soon to give birth to her own.
She had thought her work was done,

having been alone for such a long time.

Best to Leave Creek in the Woods

Tell instead about a swollen flow
from last night's deluge, swill of bubbles spilling
between two rocks, a trill and glissando
as water rushes downstream.

Skip the word *rocks.* Pinpoint that single chunk
in the bend, chiseled into a granite chalice,
catching not *leaves,* but—count them—one, two, three
brown willow oaks and one dogwood tinged

in *red*—no, make that russet, autumn's residue.
And since you've introduced the seasons,
let it be spring with a splash of peonies on the bank,
bright-white bobbleheads, their petals

dappled in blood, folding in on themselves,
heavy with nectar and the haunt of black ants.
Whittle the words to their essence—from *bird*
to white-throated sparrow, your favorite, or

brown-crested flycatcher. Even that dull house wren
you saw last summer feeding her hatchlings
in—not a *pot,* but a terra-cotta planter,
60-gallon. All morning you watched her

flit out and back, perching on a stone wall before
swooping in, her mouth brimming worm-green.
And then the moment you knew, though
a double-glass door muffled the sound,

she had paused too long. Stock-still that mother,
her jaw a loosened hinge. Inside the clay pot,
unspeakable, that thick black coil,
her wild unlit eye groping the nest.

Sunflowers

in Umbria, late summer

If not for the bosque of olive trees
on every hill, leaves winking glitter,

the rows of unplucked grapevines
heavy with wishes of wine,

so many tilled fields of brown dirt
resting for the next season.

If not for the acres of yellow faces,
tipping their heads up to follow the sun.

Though, standing barefoot in dewy grass,
I confess that I came too late

to the bloom, only dapples peaking by now
through black bowed heads.

Here is where I gather what's left.
Olives, yes these olives, and the blood of red

grapes—sangiovese grosso, sangioveto—low
echo of a rooster's call on the stone wall

of an old farmhouse I've rented,
clouds folding into their own shadows

untucking the daylight. If not for these,
and the harvest to come—birdseed and tasty oil,

the heartbreak of all the yellow
that might have been, the dazzle, the burn.

Farm to Table, a Blessing

Blue Hill Stone Barn Farm, Hudson River Valley

No matter these hasty blossoms
of cherry and redbud, the valley
still in winter. Tonight we'll welcome the last
of its root vegetables—beets, carrots,
sunchokes, parsnips. What the land has given up,
      we forage: root, leaf, stem. Dig beneath
the muck soil for onions, and along the tended rows
spring seedlings in their cycle of moon and season.

Below the tender plantings,
          our ancient source of watershed
flowing through stone and aqueduct, and deeper still
this valley's bedrock—limestone and shale. In that shale
      a yearning so fierce, some would coax it out
with untold thrashing, let loose a residue stew
of heat-trapping gas, tainted groundwater,
      an ache in our lungs.

How to harness our hunger
for it all. The riches beneath us,
yet this too—soft pastures where livestock graze
and Rhode Island reds run free, gracing our plate
      with a panko-crusted soft-boiled egg,
      a scoop of blood sausage,
paired with a glass of burgundy or barolo,
chilled water from the tap.

Baking Chicken Pie with My Mother

*after tracking down her recipe,
handwritten on a yellowed 3x5 index card*

Regular pastry for a two-crust pie
*so why not make it irregular
for once, Mom, then we can*
Boil the chicken in salt water
*while guessing how much chicken and how the hell
much salt did it take for you to stay married those 50 years,
before we have to*
Pull the chicken from its skin and bones
*and there you were, skin and bones in the end,
neither of us ready to*
Put the chicken in the pastry
*but this time we won't save the breast for him,
instead we'll*
Cook it until tender
*like that year in 9th grade when you took me shopping
for a broken heart but all I needed was a hug—so let's*
Sprinkle a little flour and pepper on it
Pour a little broth over it
*a little of this, a little of that—how little
I knew you, how much I wish we could have*
Put some water on the top crust to make it stick better
*like a baptism, like a blessing for my granddaughter,
born on your 100th. Is that you behind her blue eyes?
Time now to*
Cut a few slits in the top
*to let out some steam, Helen, may I call you Helen,
then together we'll*
Bake it until the crust is brown
Slice and serve with warm broth

Last Meal, Death Row

in response to artist Julie Green's depiction of
600 selected last suppers, painted blue on white plates

It was the night of lobster in drawn butter.
Ice water in a cold glass. It was the last night
of excuses. A night of cigarettes and soda.
An apple to clear a bad taste on a tongue.
It was a mother allowed in the prison kitchen boiling up
chicken and dumplings for her son. It was a choice, first
in a long time. It was a birthday cake, first ever.
It was a night of sacalait fish topped with crawfish étouffée.
A night of strawberries and cream. Steak and fries.
It was a night of no meal. Superstitious. Chance
of a pardon, he'd say. It was the night of his last hunger.
Four olives. A jar of dill pickles. Bowl of black walnut
ice cream, sugar free. None for her, thank you,
but a large meat pizza delivered to a homeless man
on the street. Nameless. And for the named—Odell, Ted,
Ricky Ray, Teresa, Ignacio, Timothy, Velma—twice-baked
potato with cheddar cheese, biscuits and apple butter,
a verse from God's word, three shots of Jack Daniels:
one for justice, one for equality, one for world peace.

Considering Castration

after a report that 14th-century eunuchs lived
up to twenty years longer than non-castrated males

Suppose you were the mother of a young son
called to serve the imperial court.
      You know that only the ruler

is non-*castratus*. You've heard the tales
from other kingdoms—knife to the shaft,
      testicles baited with human waste,

         clamp of a dog's bite.
But jobs are scarce and if, in hunger, your boy
has stolen a goat from the marketplace

or a pocket of plums, emasculation
         is a lesser penance than death.
Is that what you'd tell yourself?

That he may rise from treble singer
or harem guard to be
      favored by the king?

Or when drained of desire, he'll live longer?
      What about you, left with only
the scent of him whole, the grace

at his birth when you traced
every body part—ribcage and nose, curve
         of the ear, each finger and toe,

and after his bath, how slowly you'd bend
      to trim his nails with your teeth,
so careful not to let him bleed.

Barbeque Pit

We've climbed barefoot down from the hedge of evergreens.

We've washed the soles of our feet
     at the edge of the bathtub, also our scabbing knees.

We're cracking a window for something familiar.

You. Daddy. There in the backyard. Grilling a two-inch sirloin, swilling
     a double bourbon while lightning bugs flicker.

They took down the barbeque pit when we sold the house.
     (They took down the house.)

Those doves still mourn on the wire by Mother's forsythia.
     The bees have left the ligustrum.

We want the bees back, the fireflies, the mockingbird.

Even the steak you'd sear on Saturday night,
     creosote-crusted, its raw flesh too tough for us to bite.

Woman with Broken Shell

Beside her bare foot, a rippled, dappled arch
of gray shell, its edges listing in wet sand.

She picks it up, peers through its perfect pinhole
toward the dunes where a cottage might have been

and a child in pink baby doll pajamas hanging
like a spider on a door frame. Her father is lathering up,

working magic with the slip of a wrist, swish of tender
bristles nuzzling her face, sweet smell of cold

eucalyptus. Sometimes the razor nicks his skin till he bleeds.
Sometimes she lifts up the rift of time, always

light settling somewhere on white venetian blinds,
always the beach white and fine-grained.

Flanked by florescence, she tosses her shell
back to the sea, ragamuffin sacrifice of broken bone.

Beyond the foam, an old man fishing on a pier,
the pier still riding the tide.

Linger of Salt and Bone

Even if I were a blind person, tapping
my red-tipped stick toward a path through
ocean dunes, I'd know by the smell
it's garbage day on Hatteras Island. Stinking hulls
and fishy bones fill the cans of cottages, proof
that guests have downed a week's worth
from the sea, leaving their leavings for me
                              to remember

                    *

that time our dog Pinto rolled on a dead fish
at Kitty Hawk just as we were packing the car
        to go home,
                how my mother hosed her off,
but even now...

                    *

Note to the weekly renters: So you there in the *SunPhun,*
Ocean Motion and *For the Halibut.* Extravagance
comes to mind.
Indulgence.
Excess.
Gluttony.
Insatiability.
Loneliness.

                    *

Maybe it was a family reunion you were having, a last fling
before a son goes to college, old girlfriends single again
or cancer-free—and ravenous?

                    *

Marcel Proust wrote, "taste and smell alone, more fragile
but enduring...remain poised a long time, like souls...
and bear unflinchingly, in the tiny...drop of their essence,
the vast structure of recollection."

                    *

So what if I, solo traveler, once had my essence ripped
to shreds, raw flesh hanging like a hooked fish.
Go ahead and weigh me.
Take home the damn trophy.
But don't make me drift in your bliss.

                    *

Or simply this: the hippocampus is connected
to the olfactory nerve (as the shin bone's connected
to the ankle bone—and I'm eight years old again).

*

Note to Ishmael: What was it like on the Pequod,
its rail and deck trimmed in stench: mackerel guts,
shrimp heads, plankton, krill. All the while, catch
after catch, Ahab would hold out for the big one,
wishing it sliced and emptied, filling the bilge
with odiferous doom.

*

Boil till they float to the surface.
Clean out the feces with a knife.
Pop and suck the heads.
Scrape off the scales.
Cut open the innards.
Twist off the claws.
Crack the back and
squeeze out the meat with your teeth.
I'm thinking about the cracking of bones.

*

And that whalebone left to rot
on the novel's bow, in the captain's dreams,
        its jaw the sieve of the sea, eighteen feet
of cone-shaped daggers, blubber stripped,
            picked clean by gulls, delicious jubilee.

*

What could be more lonely than a beached whale,
the one everyone tries to save. Bucket
after bucket full of water, what they think
he needs, no clue he may be hungry.

*

And one's essence?
Pluff-mud between my toes. Cord grass tickling
knobby knees. Croakers, drums, and menhaden gone
as the marsh empties.
        A mullet leaps.

Fiddler crabs and snails burrow to keep cool.
The blue heron waits. Mussels and oysters wait.
Bouquet of low tide on an inland breeze—chlorophyll,
animal decay. A father tilts his bait bucket to teach
this barefoot child how to smell the salt.

Alibi

According to New Hampshire legend, in 1891 a young husband went out one night, returning 39 years later claiming only a vague notion of California, Panama, and Cuba

A young man went out after supper. His wife washed the dishes, lit a candle in a window, went to bed. *Where did you go,* she asked when he returned thirty-nine years later. *Once a gray moth lit on the end of my finger,* he said. *What was her name,* she asked. He said he didn't know but moonlight billowed her wings like flame. *Brighter than my candle,* she asked, *the one I lit every night in the window? The moth was the candle I followed,* he said. *I guess there were too many roads out. What roads,* she asked. *Footbridges, railroad grades, brooks cascading past narrow flumes. You're telling me you walked in waterfalls without your boots?* He said it was the ancestors calling him to pound their dirt into trails, to lie down in the valley of their lust. *Why would you lie in the dirt,* she asked. *Something about the common milkweed,* he said, *the hobblebush, wild lupine, forsaking them for purple fruits, mangroves, monkey flowers. What do you know about monkey flowers,* she asked, *and what did you think the neighbors would say? We'll be the talk of legend,* he said, *so someday years from now tourists will settle in wood chairs at the edge of Lake Winnipesaukee, imagining our tale. But it's already years from now, thirty-nine to be exact, and what if I'm dead by the time you return?* He hadn't thought about that, he said. He went to the window to light a candle, though he didn't remember her going out.

It Is Snowing

They sit in his red mustang
in front of her dorm.
He asks if he can kiss her
and she says yes.
She doesn't open her mouth.

They talk for hours. It is snowing.
They are barely twenty. Four years
since her high school boyfriend
dropped her
for a cheerleader.
Five years since his mother
killed herself
while he was off in boarding school.
Six months since
he swore off chasing wild girls.

Snow banks a slope on the curb
outside his car. Their breath
has fogged the windows.
No one thinks to do the math.

The L Word

Before the word dared be spoken,
the word that means more than making love or love
how you make me laugh, the word

that catches in superstition's net—an old lover's
cheatin' heart, havoc of shadow and light.

Before that, he brought her odd gifts.
A six-ounce jar of Lingonberry jam,
mellowed, it said on the label, *under a midnight sun,*

sun that never wanders, making the berries promise
to both nip and kiss the tongue.

Two records—early reggae, some Texas ballads,
their ripe lyrics about cowboys and fair lovers
wandering among parched olive trees

under luminescence of lavender-gray.
Titillating. Tart. If that's not love, she thought.

And a card, handmade, about a lonely tree. Blue spruce.
So blue, it made her think he must have known
her gypsy past—how, in time, if cornered, she'd bite.

The tree's needles, in cross section, stiff and prickly.
In sunlight, effervescent as diamonds.

Engagement Ring, Gone Missing

From the day his goofy clues led her
to a dazzle in the glove box
of his car, she never took it off.

Never. Until he bolted years later
to poke around the edge of an ache
she couldn't ease. It was then she stashed it

in the chest-on-chest they had shared,
an heirloom they could barely afford
when they were still destitute with love.

Eventually he returned, though
she never found the ring. Yes, he would
replace it. Yes, in a decade he'd leave again.

And yes, sometimes even now—irascible itch
that won't stay scratched—she'll catch herself
riffling through the clothes

in that chest-on-chest, scouring the corners
of its old mahogany drawers, cracks
in the slats, the rough bevels beneath.

To the Roses of Kenya

after ethnic violence threatens the export
of millions of fresh-cut flowers, mainly roses

In a country where the earth runs hot,
it's your nature to bloom.

When the land is strangled and no one
comes to tend you, you bloom.

In shadow of ethnic grooming, your pickers
consumed by fear, their houses torched,

and yet you bloom scarlet-rouge.
How can you bear such beauty?

Your fields torn,
armed guards called in to clip your stems,

shelter your petals, airlift you out
by moonlight,

and you bloom.
February looming.

You know the lovelorn depend on you.
You know the torment of thorns.

Blue in Winter, Blame the Moon

after a New York Times article on biological rhythms,
peppered with phrases from the dining section

Blue in winter, blame the moon, say the scientists
for anyone living dark in the northern latitudes.

Overeating, sleeping in fits, activity cycles
shifted—even for mutant hamsters and fruit flies.

We trudge through cabbage season, tongue tingling
at the thought of gumbo and Sazerac, more laissez-faire

than the fusty French. Earth spins and the moon
thumps inside our cells. Trillions of clocks, ticking, ticking.

The universe feels it. Some cataclysm must have caused
our nights to topple like this, seasons spliced

like a butchered hog. We're a mélange of earth crust
and asteroid dust—yes, *that* asteroid,

ejected into space, congealing as moon, tilting
primordial earth. We are orbs of something

we can't quite claim. A recipe for stardust.
Chickpeas coming home to roost.

Salty-Sour-Bitter-Sweet

The highlight is my falafel
     she says over lunch, arousing our tongues, not
for the taste of garlic and fried fava beans, fritters on lafa,
but for the succulence of her syllables.

Stop reading and say it: the highlight is my falafel,
the highlight is my falafel. Now taste it.

Like the way a rose-breasted grosbeak
might taste the glow when hearing his name—
rose-breasted grosbeak—prodding a song more mellow
     than a common robin's.

Or over there in the garden border,
               beneath the bird's perch,

summer's growth of—listen to it—rosemary,
rhododendron, and by the stone wall a lonely mimosa,
its dawn-hued shoots
     blooming sooner this season,

shade and scent easing
          into the troughs of our tongue buds,

lying down
     with falafel's familiar linger.
Olive oil, coriander, cumin, and that dazzling startle
of tahini drizzle on our lips.

Coming in June

Up through dark burrows they'll quiver,
then strip off dry husks, leaving them
clinging to tree bark or window screens.
Uncountable brood, red-blazed eyes,
throbbing their sexual song.
What they'll not do
is ponder, pray liturgies, bend
bloody-kneed beneath ancient creeds,
        I believe I believe I believe.

For seventeen years they've hunkered
in deep hush, sucking root juices,
making way for a sultry stir
low in their bellies.
Amorous as muscled gods.
                Mate. Mate. Mate.
Love as epitaph. And the afterlife?
A muted summer porch, an unlatched
screen door, sky inflamed
with constellations, the earth quiet again.

But truth be told, it's hard for me to go back
to a muted porch, screen door choked
in honeysuckle, no matter this frenzy
to rise out of a bruised ground.
Too many lonely summer nights.
Therapists have made fortunes over
songs like theirs:
        I only have eyes...
I'm nothing if not...
                I'd give up my life for you.

One thing on their minds for sure,
these giant bugs—a shiver, a swig
of holy intoxication. And then they die.
        Maybe it's best.

"I Went There with My Boyfriend at the Time," We Overhear a Woman Say as We Pass Her in the Park

Not to be confused with current boyfriend
or one-and-only, so I wonder at what *time* exactly
and with which *boyfriend:* first or fifteenth
and where was *there:* a cruise to Mexico,
shopping spree at Tiffany's or
a therapy session on miscommunication?
How old was he, the *boyfriend at the time:*
sixteen twenty-eight thirty-nine, how buff how tan,
how long did he stay: a month five years,

and what would he have to say
about her, his *girlfriend at the time:* clumsy in bed, sexy
in the kitchen, and oh, dear, I'm thinking
what about us, I mean *you,*
what would you say
about your *girlfriend,* I mean *me,* and
when does it go from *girlfriend* to *girlfriend at the time*?
Have you already tasted those words in your mouth
when I'm not around, maybe in the shower
or at the office, or even now,

holding hands as we walk? I mean, we seem
to be good, don't you think, you stroking
my hair last night while we watched the news,
the wine bar Friday and a movie I chose,
but one never knows
when *girlfriend* might turn to *girlfriend at the time,*
especially the girlfriend, oh my god,
and all the while, the boyfriend might simply
be upping his guts, notching his belt,
fleshing out some tales of their time together
so she'll have something
to talk about after he goes.

Trust Fall

Scent on the pillow still you
your toothbrush left in a bathroom drawer
echo of urging unheard   yet

not a shock you'd leave one day
those wicked words we tribute to hearts
opened and *broken*

or maybe that game at camp
between bonfire and Taps   how fluid my body
to learn how good it felt to be touched

back of the neck and hairline
brush of a nipple through my knit shirt
everyone crossing arms

planting feet in the dirt   backs straight
eyes shut   again and again falling
stiff into the grasp of fellow campers

hearts thumping   everyone
caught by everyone   until one night
I was not   blood burning

arousal rising   as I waited   for those fingers
on my skin   and though his name
eludes me now   the night remembers

a crescent moon slicing clouds
into rain   spatter of wet red clay on my
bare ankles   a strange smell of rust

II

If I put my face to the glass
I can make out the ghost.

from *One with Others*
C. D. Wright

By the Window at Dawn, I Think of Color

for Esther

Faint outline of the house next door,
wrought-iron fence, border of hollies, as pink
pools from a daybreak sky. More pallid than pink,

I'm thinking *flesh,* that one inexcusable color
in the box of Crayolas we learned from.

Long after we knew our primaries, my brother
would frame that crayon, hang it
on a bathroom wall as parody. To a woman

who lived on a street without fences or curbs
it was anything but jest. Did she, I wonder, before

becoming our family maid, spend her childhood
reworking that label to

    mocha, mahogany, cinnamon, bark?

When denied a seat at my country club wedding reception,
she sent blue hydrangeas instead, picked from her patch
of hardscrabble dirt a million miles away.

    Forty years—and still those flowers.

Blue as the sky as it blooms this morning out the window,
lighting my place on the planet. By now, I see the blister

of red and yellow maples, the neighbor's shutters
and downspouts, a back door cracked just enough
for the dogs to come and go.

Fish Camp, Indian River, 1956

I'm the one you see with the bony legs
and new frizzy perm, the one scuffling
        with my brother outside our shabby cabin
while our parents cast fishing lines

into the greasy river,
        me hopping to balance on one foot
while trying to pull a sandspur
out of the other, good heel coming down hard

on more stickers, falling on my knees, knees
that'll be stuck and scabbed the whole vacation,
        here where conch shell
ashtrays clutter the porch and mosquitoes

gnaw holes in our screens, while my friends
        have gone to a Holiday Inn
or maybe even the Waldorf Astoria
in New York City and I'm the one

in a hole hot as hell, the one whose skin
will tan dark this summer
        so back home everyone will say,
Wow, you sure are black, and

I'll smile because it's a good thing, and
it won't be until much later that I'll find out
what I was that summer was not black at all
        but very very white, in fact so white

I might one day opt out of such a dreary place
reeking of fish bait, waitress in the diner
        sopping hotcakes with cane syrup,
thick and bitter as the river, might choose,

if I wanted, to stay at a motel with a fancy
swimming pool, even join some highfalutin
        country club where I'd know
that, deserved or not, they'd let me in.

Dentist's Office, 1955

This much I can tell you: that ladies
would dress to go downtown, mothers

all girdled up and gartered, young ones
bound in shiny shoes with buckle straps,

that the Reynolds Building smelled oily and dark,
and the man steering the wooden elevator

to the third floor, whipping
that cage shut with a *good morning ma'am,*

had skin the color of swamp water
and gaps in his teeth,

and that, when I'd spit into the basin,
my head still banging from the drill, wasted

slivers of silver would glitter like little fish
swimming round and round

in their white porcelain bowl.

Tabula Rasa

It never snows down south
that I don't go back
to those three white Wednesdays in March,
each one shrouded with a smooth
layer of grace, our world pure
as a bare calendar page.
It was early '60s. Every night I'd bundle
with friends by a barrel of bonfire
on the country club's steepest fairway,
all our snug brick houses
an arm's orbit away,
school an easy trade-in
for hot chocolate and a fast sled.

Each week, another frozen surprise
till we learned to count on it.
Unmitigated radiance
that became our status quo,
our cosmology,
our holy of holies—as if this life
would surely go on without a hitch.

We Always Called Him Fletcher

Never by his first name, Albert, or Mr. Fletcher.
He was tall as a sugar pine, skin the color

of freckled walnuts, walked our whole
neighborhood, hauling

an extension ladder from job to job,
his back straight as gospel.

I knew nothing beyond
his easy manners and that one

summer morning when I rode with my dad
to snag him from the Shell Station

where he managed to unfold
from a lean-to out back, tools in tow.

There were white lies about Fletcher.
His imagined gratitude for a bologna sandwich

served on our back porch stoop, water
from the spigot. Small wad of bills

for a day's work, a gracious plenty. Even
my mother's word to name him was skewed.

Negra. The way she'd let the long O slide
between proper and implication. Nobody spoke

of the little shed or the cot I saw tucked
in the back, instead let me believe

what was easy—a respite after a long walk
from home, an early breakfast

of eggs and grits with his family,
kids watching cartoons before camp,

wife dressing to do what women do,
church circle or bridge at the club.

Only a Boy Back Then

Actually it's the truth, she says to the man
who was a boy back then, the boy
who was in her high school
though she never saw him. She never
saw him in school, she says, or at the drug store
where she'd go for a Saturday hotdog with friends.
She never saw him at the movies downtown
where he tells her he'd wait
outside on the sidewalk
at the door she never saw,
holding his sack of popcorn popped
from home by his mother, waiting to give his dime
to the ticket-taker who'd nod him
and his brothers and sisters
up three dark flights to a balcony
she never knew was there. She tells him now
she never knew it was there, she never knew
his friends would lean over the rail to watch
the kids below, bolt back to their seats
if anyone turned around or looked up.
We must have seen the same movies, she says
but that really doesn't matter now, does it?
What matters is this, she tells the man, and *yes,*
actually, it's the truth. She never turned around.
She never looked up.

What I Remember Most about God

is that spark in her eye when she'd say
Cut yourself some slack there, girl,
how she'd set her mouth all crooked
and lean into my face like she knew something I didn't
but was about to find out. What I remember most about God
is that her neck had wrinkles, her breasts sagged,
and her breath smelled like Blenheim ginger ale. And the tales
she told of her misadventures, OMG, that's what I remember
most: Days she'd lie in a feather hammock—no
sunscreen, polka dots stippling her nose. Travels
untraveled. Souls unsaved. Shelves of books, not even
dog-eared. (I'm not sure how she got the job.)
And the hours she'd spend crafting poems—even a novel once—
that flickered into mist by morning.

What I remember most about God is her lush garden
by the gate—lavender and hydrangeas *made blue*
out of missed wishes (her words)—and the way
she could look me up and down and ask,
Now what were you saying, Sweetheart?

Fishing in White Lace

after a National Geographic photograph by David Alan
Harvey of a young woman fishing on a Nags Head pier

Why this pier   and you in a lacy white dress
when most would be
        in T-shirts and cutoff jeans
and alone at night   or is it dawn   no light breaking

            the thin line between sea and sky
purple backdrop   flat   dark
        and a rough rail in shadow

Yet there you glow   in icy shimmer
        blinding in the contrast   white
broken only by a blue satin ribbon cinched at your waist
            your hem fluttering
at the curve of your knee

Light emits from within   Maybe you're a spirit
standing bold in soft cotton   your black braid
        burning a heart line down your back
head turned slightly   as if searching for something
        evening star   beacon for incoming boats   a new truth

your rod lifted high over the rail   no bend
to sense struggle   yet   what might evolve
        flesh on your line   heat and fire   a red and salty climax
whatever we make your story to be

On Attending a Commemoration
of the 1964 Civil Rights Act, I Come Home
to Find a Bat in My Bedroom

Top of the stairs, feeling for the light switch
in a dark room—this instead—darting,

swooping past my hair, my left ear, my right.
Not the chimney swift I would have favored

or a gentle house wren, something easily
gathered in a soft cloth or coaxed out

the back door. This one's wingspan is
too wide, too fluid. A dark shadow

I can't navigate, nor my thoughts—
a shrunken head with teeth, the dreaded

bite, how would I sleep? I back out
of the room, consider then my toothbrush

and bedsheets fresh from the dryer,
reenter with an old towel and broom.

I don't know if fear can justify
the tiny thing he'd become, no bigger

on the floor than a man's thumb. Lurking
no longer on my doorframe, blind

gaze ablaze in his own angst, both of us
turned strangers backed into corners,

one poised for preservation, the other
caught in someone else's status quo.

So here I am, here he is, limp tatter
of rag, wings tucked into submission,

folded small and neat and proper as if
making one last effort to please.

March on Washington, 50th Anniversary

Technicolor on TV this time—but look
hard among the chromatic thousands
for the ones who will forever

inescapably be black and white.
They too are marching today: men with dogs
and hoses, four little girls in a church,

that fiery bus full of students riding
for something called freedom.
And Esther, who, on this day, would set

her ironing aside, perch on a footstool
to watch. My brother, barely eleven,
entering our small den from school,

saw her face wet and twisted. He was
scared, confused. No one
had warned him about this.

All will be better now, she said, and he,
knowing she was someone he could trust,
sat down beside her to wait.

Meditations on a Snowman

Day four from the blizzard
        his head is toppled
scarf and straw sombrero
        on an ice-capped sidewalk crust

in a young boy's yard
        young boy back to school
but before the bus
        a reconfiguration

On day six
        the head undone again
and with it—ears eyes mouth
        tongue teeth intimations

of a child's wild faith—
        all that's left
of a shrunken torso
        melt and bungle now

What is life's core anyway
        age-old wonder
head with gears and rigging
        or a body's swish

of heart and gut
        The robins are out
for worms today—
        ask them—

and the new green shoots
        poking from crocus bulbs
follow their map
        or quiz this ramshackle fellow

now settled in a warm puddle
        clinging to his last tatters
dirty snow and what was once
        a fine floppy hat

Urban Renewal

As the crickets' soft autumn hum/is to us
so are we to the trees/they are
to the rocks and the hill
　　　　　　　　　—Gary Snyder

So what if we drain the koi pond
in our new yard, relocate the orange fish,

cover the breach with treated wood
to make the children safe, all good.

But here's the thing: the bullfrog.

Like a relic, he squats on the concrete walk
as we watch him, inches from what yesterday
was a hop and a splash home.

Of course we'll scoop him up, deliver him kindly
to join the koi down the street. But what if

it's true that no matter the landscape—piney woods,
rain forest, backyard or field—there beats

a signature symphony. Reptiles, mammals,
birds and bugs, even wind in the trees
and ripples on a murky puddle.

Until something shifts.
　　　Does the bullfrog know
　　　what goes when he goes?

His low-toned bass plucked against lily pads,
harmonizing a syncopation of crickets,
a barred owl's lyric.

And for those with the oldest haunts—slam
of a screen door, shuffle of gin-rummy cards
on a rickety table, kids spitting seeds into buckets

ping ping ping in the orbit that once was,
wild honeysuckle vine growing so fast,
　　　they'd swear they could hear it sing.

Male Olive Ridley Sea Turtle Hanging Dead

after a National Geographic photo by Bill Curtsinger
of a longline set for the shark fin soup trade

He's old as myth, this random scrap
snagged in a fisherman's trap,

his underbelly glacial green, immortal
bloom, embalmed in blue salt.

The body fills the photograph,
neck and legs in dangle, hanging limp.

Behind and beyond for sixty miles
of longline filament—I have to tell

the whole story—hundreds more
like him, and seabirds

caught by the glint of rusting hooks,
and mangled sharks left drifting

for the take of their fins.
I think he would want us to know

he's not alone, though
all we see, all we feel is the pull

of this one lone turtle. His last graceful
stroke before struggle, surrender.

On his way to nesting grounds.
Seed for a thousand eggs.

While Trying to Let Go of the Dying Sea Lions, I Find Myself Addressing my Ex-Husband

Water warmer now, minnows gone deeper toward
cooler seas. Let go of the minnows.

Let go of the sea lions who feed on the minnows,
deeper colder longer, while foraging for their pups.

Oh, God, let go of the pups,
weary with hunger and breathlessness, pouring

onto ocean shores ribbed and ravaged, crawling onto docks
and decks, curling into clay pots like old brown socks.

Let go of the pots and the old brown socks
and that carefree day—the two of us

drifting down the Florida coast, camp stove and tent in tow,
abundant with time and the newness of each other.

Let go of time and the tent in tow and stopping
for anything—fresh-squeezed orange juice, monkey jungle,

a sign that lured us in to swim with the dolphins.
Stopping, swimming, dripping wet in a shell-and-gift shop,

shocked to see a pet sea lion skid across the tile
to slide under a counter where we stood.

It was then I thought I would love you forever,
our feet puddled in cold salty water, laughter ricocheting

off cinderblock walls, that jokester's throaty bark,
a punch line that still knocks me dead.

Buttered Grits

Ellen Smith Craft, born of slave and white owner, fled Georgia with her new husband in 1848. They traveled by foot, train and ship to Boston and England before returning to the South to build a farm and school for freed slaves.

It was Christmastime, old moon burning full and hard
through the pines, same as it did the night I was born,
Mama said—said it was that moon turned my skin white,

got us sold to a place in Macon and me sent to the big house
at twelve, with all those books and maps of cities
long past our rutted red clay fields. So there we were,

him and me, walking north, resting in some stranger's woods,
my stolen hat tossed on the edge of a rock—wide-rimmed,
that hat, brown silk and plucked pheasant feathers.

Tired as leftovers, I leaned my back against a locust tree's
rough bark, let his nappy head settle in my lap,
me there lifting those velveteen skirts

so he could rub his hands up and down my yellow legs.
Buttered grits, he called my skin—*skin that'll carry us out,*
he'd say. And what an easy stealing it was.

Mistress's hat and dress passed with supper's trash,
him waiting in the shadows, us chasing the tail of a night sky
toward the road, walking proper and distant,

me keeping a sharp step ahead of him, all the while him
bowing and nodding till we'd crossed that line, still masking
as something he's not, never was, never will be again.

What If the Mad Farmer Could Sit In
at a New Year's Day Potluck
during a Global Recession

after Wendell Berry

Talk turns from black-eyed peas and collards
to banks closing and governments falling on their knees.
One man's fix—a gated farm with cattle and swine,

a hired hand to tend the land, airstrip for the pilot
in the clan, a pot of chicken stew simmering on a stove,
cellar stocked with wine.

What was it Orwell said about some animals
being more equal than others? What to bow down to
but bomb shelters and moated castles,

hunkering holy behind barbed wire and wrought iron.
They'll plow acres into perfect rows, the planet
already hot enough to crack stones.

Tonight the mad farmer dreams
of planting trees, peeing fine champagne into a river.
From nowhere—a field of black soil. He stoops

to load his mule cart, crosses a rickety plank bridge
to a shantytown of dust and dung, dozens
of faceless men, their hands reaching for the shovel.

Homeless

for Bill Bailey

His hands are red
and barnacled from winter
on the streets, knuckled
hard on the handlebars of his bike
as he waits in line for soup.
I think about red canyon walls I saw once
reaching up to southwest sky like hope.
I ask what keeps him from going there.
Bicycle needs welding, he says,
and even so, they won't give us gloves
until Christmas.

Naming the Snake

When someone has slit the throat
of a black snake on a hot sidewalk.

When downtown near a small cafe a woman
all bluster, limp twist of scorn and shame.

Limp twist of soft underbelly, the snake
when its throat is slit by someone raging.

When a woman is begging surrender,
begging to use the cafe's bathroom.
So too the snake, begging to skim into dry thicket

in July heat, crossing a sidewalk toward a creek bed
when blackberries swell the bank.

When downtown, a cafe owner
rages scorn and shame on a woman
who crosses a sidewalk toward him.

Simple woman, simple
black snake, rat snake, pilot racer.

Who is he to think he knows my name?
Tattered backpack, crook in my walk, color of my skin?

Black as a snake slit on a sidewalk
when every July, in shadows of dry thicket,
blackberries swell the bank.

Soft underbelly begging surrender,
crossing to beg for a bathroom—tattered, crooked

woman, skimming toward a creek bed,
crossing a hot sidewalk.

Pink Clock Radio

Has the world gone crazy, somebody asks
in our weekly dialogue on Faith and Doubt.

Blood in the streets, young men on their knees,
even old women—evangelicals blaming it on
original sin, half the citizens blaming it
on the guns, half on the gays.

What really happened in the garden, I wonder,
that snake taking the rap while God wrote scripture

that would one day confuse his constituents.
Night after night I'd watch my broken father stare
from a whisky bottle through a picture window into
our dark backyard. No doubt decades later I'd wish

I could bring us back to a Christmas morning when
his present for me under the tree was exactly

what I had asked him for—a pink clock radio
for my bedside table, a time in that bare flash
when faith was as real to me
as it might have been in the garden

if God had had the wherewithal and grace
to let the snake just be a snake.

Lunch at the Pink Elephant, Old Girlfriends

Boca Grande, Florida

And so we've come for the codfish, lightly battered,
served on a soft roll. Or the signature Pink Cobb
with baby greens and arugula.

Next to us on the patio, a tableful of old men
eating grilled cheese and French fries, off-menu.

When we quiz the waitress,
she tells us *they've been coming here for twenty-five years.*
        Plus, they asked.

We order the same childhood staple, two rounds
with extra fries, eat every bite.

        Who are you?
we ask the men as they pass our table to leave.
P.I.P.s, they say. *Previously Important People.*

We laugh, then ramble back decades
to where we started. Nine southern gals in compliance

and platitudes, growing up in the '50s with hopes
for husbands and big breasts. By now we know
what thrives. Breeze off the gulf.

Crushed oyster shells under our feet.
This salty taste of cheddar on white bread.

This Is Not a Fairy Tale

> "My House"
> You make me cozy
> You keep me so warm
> You are the only house I want
>   —Jasmin Perez Lopez

Once there was a young girl who walked
a wooded path on her way home from school.
This is not a fairy tale.

A stranger walking the same woods days later
spotted a poem handwritten on yellow paper,
slipped perhaps from a young girl's bookbag.

The stranger was not a witch but a woman
who picked up the paper, thin and dingy
from the soles of running shoes
and pockmarked with twigs and gravel.

The title was underlined, the poem unpunctuated.
From its tidy block letters the woman pictured
a second grader and, from the name on the poem,
a girl with brown eyes and brown skin.

The woman tucked the poem into her satchel
where it would stay for many days and many nights.
This is not a fable. This is not a parable. But when

there comes a time of fear in the hearts of families,
the woman, this stranger, will take out the poem,
reread the girl's words she had shielded
for so long from goblins and fools.

It is then she'll wish she could make a bargain
with a mirror on a wall for this girl she'll never
know, this girl writing at a desk somewhere, in a house

somewhere, maybe in that same house, the only one
she ever wanted, the house that once upon a time
made the girl cozy and kept her so warm.

Same Old Ghost in the Basement

After coming cross-country
and no one to greet her and nothing

in the pantry but a fruitcake from last Christmas
and a cracked wine glass in the sink

she sat down in a not-so-easy chair
to read *Charlotte's Web* for the umpteenth time.
        She knew she'd cry.

Endings are harder to clean up
than a tumbler of spilled toothpicks.
Damn that spider! Damn the hangnail

on her big toe. Damn the way you can't
buy curtains for a round window.

(She'd forgotten this place was full of
round windows.)

And on the sideboard next to
the silver service that was always tarnished
a vase of unpetaled petunias.

What had she expected?
        Yellow roses? Fireflies in a mason jar?

Once There Was a Field

of buttercups
on the corner of Plymouth and Country Club
a cut-through on the path
to grade school
    a field that seemed to go on forever
    the way one bloom
    if held close to the chin
        could light a child's face

III

Out beyond ideas
of wrongdoing and rightdoing,
there is a field. I'll meet you there.

—Rumi

Furnace Busted, I Think of the Dead

for Queenie, a typhoon survivor

Bone-cold in this early freeze
not yet November rain and wind scorning through icy
windowpanes making the chill bitter inside my house

Legs ache from fighting the shivers as I wait

for a repairman
I own a closet full of coats gloves hats
Hot water heater   Car   Library card

Don't have to be cold

No water rages through my door
house filling
with shrimp and fish from a broken vessel at the dock
and my father miles off the coast counting

the cost of ditching his fishing boat
as waves slam against his hull
My one-legged grandfather doesn't need to be toted
to higher ground

I don't even have
a one-legged grandfather

Flies won't gather on garbage in my street

I'll not be digging through
rubble dragging body bags
to a makeshift morgue

All my memories are dry
tucked in attic boxes
After supper I'll not be that girl

who clutches the back of her neck
feels herself, she says, so quickly getting thinner

Unconformity

a gap in earth's geological strata, when fossils are lost,
as in the Grand Canyon

Three days in a row, tornadoes
        have torn up the Midwest, twisted
routine into rebar, trapped

the children. A blanket of grit
        flattens roads and houses, wraps
them in conversations caught mid-breath

while the storm sabotages promise,
        burns vows to cinder. Unbidden gaps
in what might have been our evermore.

                        *

I think of that summer in the canyon, when
        we watched the pop of moon
shoot over ancient red rock walls,

touched five billion years
        of limestone, sandstone, shale, basalt,
layered and relayered.

Rocks that speak in rhythms older
        than Greek or Hebrew.
Supai, Redwall, Toroweap, Kaibab, Vishnu Schist.

Anointed names. Riddled with rain, worn by wind,
        shifted by river's rage.
Lizard's refuge now.

                        *

We hiked to a feminine place, a deep
        pink passage chiseled
by water flow into a fragile furrow,

trickle spilling into a still pool. We stepped in, rubbed
        fingers over what felt like skin.
Talcum and sage. We are carved from this.

                        *

And from this—a random tempest whisking up
        our status quo.
Chewing on metal and wood.

Horses spinning through air like loose spittle.
        Bones woven in webs of tangle.
All one can do is wander the rubble

until the sun flares wild again and
        barely visible in a bruised sky—
that same moon breaking through.

Cows Waiting in an Irish Field

They lie in clusters under a shade tree
on the round of a hill, waiting.
They stand by the rock wall
munching tufts of grass, waiting.
Where bards and druids
once called up spirits from the Otherworld,
stacked stones in faith,
sang from the bitter edges,
they bellow and wait—black, dun,
red and roan. They wait
for the rain to fill the water trough,
for the farmer to haul out hay or silage,
for the farmer to lead them away.
They all have tags in their ears.
We all have tags in our ears.
We wait for the next plate of fish and chips,
steak pie, smoked salmon on scones
with cream cheese and berry jam.
A pint of ale to settle our faith
as we sing, as we gather stones.

Rack of Lamb

imagined after a New York Times investigation

A masterpiece, the way the chef has sheared
the meat, the fat, the cartilage from its ribs.

This much I know. Raw shank rubbed with
kosher salt, virgin garlic, seared in a cast-iron skillet,
fat side roasted brown. The way bare bone shimmers
in candlelight, bidding me to bow down, every cell
in my body lifting to taste the first bite.

On my tongue a nursery rhyme, and in that lyric
a lamb born in a barn, suckled by its mother,
fleece as white as snow.

That would be the good news.
And the other? A terrible farm in Nebraska,

research lab tangled in tax dollars, probing
for profits, a cheaper meal the market's holy grail.
Pigs. Cows. I'll spare the gloom. But the lambs
in fields without sheepfold or shepherd,
an enterprise called *Easy Care*.

What does a lamb know of easy? Or profit? For this one
on my platter, what matters if he's slathered in
whole-grain mustard and pomegranate molasses?

A waiter fills my glass with a rich red Bordeaux,
perfect pairing for lamb, he says. *Notice the notes,* he says,
of blackberries spiced with earth.

I drink to the blackberries, the earth, the barn, the lamb,
the little lamb's mother in fields of green.

I drink to Mary, to this delicacy
set before me, to those children playing.

A Potter Tries to Explain Why the Day
of a Kiln Opening Is His Most Difficult

It's more than a fear of cracked pots
or the buyers' choosing. All along his dirt road,
swarms of people are gathering, waiting

for the last vessel to be lifted from the kiln, toted to a grassy field.
     Small pitchers. Forty-gallon jars.
Golden-brown beacons gleaming

in slanted sunlight. Soon, one by one on this chilly mid-fall morning
in the Carolina sand hills, lovers of his art will enter
through a sawhorse gate to choose.

He looks to the pots born of the fire.
For months he's mined the unrefined clay, worked it
with crude tools and raw hands, mixed glazes from wood ash,

    the red earth turned and burned.

Like watching a child be born, he says,
and those children's children.

He scuffs his boot as if more words might be buried
in the ground, this man
in flannel and jeans still smoky

from days of stoking the fire. From dust and heat
those children, these pots, this field
    where a fierce rapture has bloomed.

Contract

So twisted my daughter's face
as she takes her first-born for the first time.
Quivering from bliss to disbelief, then back to bliss.
For two hours they had cloistered him
coiled in wires and tubing,
watching him breathe to pink
while she waited,
space and time contorted,
her heart split like tinder
as they took him from the birthing room.
Now she is rubbing her nose
and mouth through the fuzz on his head,
tasting him with her eyes and skin, touching
each finger and toe. Like vapor
she floats above the bed,
all the while tethered to breath and bone.
She's gone past the bend in the road,
signed with a ribbon of blood.
When one day he says *you're not the boss of me*,
she'll think of this. Her song is the off-kilter lilt
of a white-throated sparrow.
No longer inside her, he is in her.

Sunset at Six Stories

A mountain town's historic basilica
     in shadow, its double-domed
crosses. Flags fluttering

on a county courthouse lawn.
     Walls of warehouse-boutiques
swabbed in amber spatter

like graffiti on old brick
     as owners scurry to their cars,
bodies bent against the season's first bluster.

Six floors up in a polished condo, a man
     reclines on a sofa. He doesn't see
the hard line of light and dark

along a cloud-train chugging across
     a sky turned plum nor two black crows
braced on a lamp post in a parking deck.

His wife of forty years, the woman
     he would have grown old with,
is dead, a new one pressing next to him.

Maples on a distant hill are grasping their last leaves,
     a random beam of sun burning
a hole through the clouds. A man

on a sofa six floors up, the woman
     he would've grown old with
dead, the new one pressing next to him,

his fingers twisted in her hair. Her impulse
     to rise, move to the desk by the window,
begin to write these words.

Fuselage

after Sabrina Tavernise,
New York Times, July 2014, Ukraine

A scattering of metal in a wheat field dotted
with flax, purple asters and Queen Anne's lace. Jagged
edge of an airline logo, a section of wing.

And bodies. Neighbors saw them after the boom,
falling silent from 30,000 feet like clumps of cloth,
some still settled in seat belts,
then strewn across crops.

A man lies naked in dark socks, left hand
crossing his chest as if pledging a vow. A teenager
decked in blue shorts, neon Nikes, limbs and neck
akimbo. A woman in a lace bra, her gray hair
woven into green pasture grass.

The reporter has walked among the dead to gather
her words, plucking them from
a sport jacket pocket, a random leather purse
sprung open by the hard landing.

I pour my second cup of green tea, fold to the jump
on page four, let her numb me with language.
Each sentence is like a nest of unbroken eggs.
I lift one, then another, each heavy as regret
in my hand. Each holding

the miscellaneous stuff of a life—
a parking ticket, tube of Nivea cream, white slippers,
a maxi pad, collection of pirate stickers,
a black bike. A limp youngster in red dirt.

I think of my grandson. A faded T-shirt
that reads *Don't Panic.* A dead parrot waving
a perfect wing. A travel guide for Bali
still sealed.

In the distance dogs are barking.
The air smells bitter.
The tea in my cup has gone cold.

Killing the Buddha

The house is empty except for an elderly cat and a woman.
The woman is listing four noble truths in a spiral notebook.
The notebook has been labeled *World Religions,*
a fresh page open for Buddhism.
      She is familiar with suffering.

Sometimes holding the pen causes a joint in her thumb
to numb. The cat has arthritis in the arch of his back.
Outside, winter birds search for seed, perch
on a fence, still as memory.
      It's been quiet in the house for too long.

A muffled thump means the cat
has jumped from the bed. Such intention, the woman
thinks, to lumber toward his litter box, the water bowl.
With a single in-breath,
      she invites peace to settle.

But the cat has rustled something.
At the far edge of the ottoman,
climbing near her left foot—a large black roach.
They all consider the consequences.
      The roach twitches.

The old cat slinks back to his place on the bed.
The woman releases her breath into the room,
clutches the notebook in both hands.
She is well-versed in the concept of reincarnation,
      decides against it.

Her in Mind

elegies for the late wife

1. Harmonic Convergence

In the beginning, I'd watch
your eyes spill, often from some lyric
on the radio or a perfect church
organ chord. *Helpless old romantic*
you'd say, though we both knew a song
had called her back—you there between us
holding loyalty in the balance, wanting
to harmonize every verse, and I,
just for once, wanting to be sung first.

2. Masquerade

At first I'd let myself wear her skin
for you to touch, but when a notion
would rise you didn't recognize, an ethic
she would never have claimed, you'd strain away,
loosen the grip you held on me.
You must have wondered who it was
you'd summoned in the dark. Some
trick of a dream whose voice
you didn't know, whose skin,
this impersonator, this phantom.

3. First Quiche

I pull out my recipe card while you
unload your tote: Julia Child, a well-worn
dish, Tupperware tub with the proper
number of dried beans for weighting down
the crust while it bakes: ten minutes
covered in buttered foil, then two,
then four uncovered. For forty-three years
you did this, you say, measurable memories
in so many kitchens, the two of you
chopping, stirring, flipping pages in Julia—
both of you savoring the flow of wine while
cooking, and she, managing to make
one glass go on forever.

Urban Book Club Gathers to Discuss
The Grand Design *by Stephen Hawking*
on the Week Higgs Boson Is Found

By God, everyone will meet at Sandy's,
though apparently the group will manifest *only if only if only if*
each can subscribe to the same
history in the same universe at the same time.
   Luckily most members are politically compatible, close in age.
    However—string theory may unravel
when it comes to sex and religion.

Sex? You know some will bring it up—we always do—still pining
  for the '60s' lawless
laws-of-nature days. I guess we could call it a top-down model
  of cosmology,
an early big bang revolution.

As for religion, some prefer science to mysticism—that familiar
apple of Adam's liking—or
as our author so wickedly dangles
in our faces as fable:

Viking wolves baying at the sun and moon.
Meddling Greek gods.
Even some obscure African deity named Bumba
who, when faced with an ache in his (or her) gut,
  simply regurgitated us all into existence.

Two Sexagenarians Strolling the Landfill
on Green Turtle Cay

and wondering *where we go* when we leave this world
of coral-packed islands floating in blue salt. Do we

rust away, dust away, shatter into shards
like those stacks of Mount Gay rum bottles,
a burned out '71 Corolla in the rubble

and, on the far ledge, a turquoise baby stroller.
(Is everything here turquoise?)

And what will we be like in the life after—a cracked
porcelain sink, empty can of WD-40, a busted
bicycle, rotted hull of a fishing skiff

or some girl's wedding dress, moth-shredded
after twenty years, silver trivets no one polished?

On the hill stands Simon, wearing ash and smudge
on his work shirt. He manages the burns when the wind
is leeward, turns mortality to smoke.

We stop to listen to wild hogs rooting
in the scrubby underbrush, sure to be

next week's bacon, and a farmer's loose chicken
darting from two local teens
with their baited cardboard trap and string.

Our aunt bet us we couldn't catch a bird,
they boast from a golf cart perch, snacking

on dry cereal from a box. A few bucks,
we figure, to get them out of her way.
Easy theology on a glitter-perfect day,

a day they don't look past.

The Last Colonoscopy

That's what the doctor divines, unless she spots
a polyp. Says I can skip the pap and mammogram,
shift to a biannual plan, check off my single shingles shot,
finally shut that door on the bane of bone scans.

Like an old dog whose body's had plenty
of prevention and prognostication,
I'll fade before most plights can take me.
If a flaw is found, we'll start a new investigation.

Meanwhile I'll dawdle under the backyard trees,
chew on a greasy bone, beg to have my ears tickled,
and conjure up a little Shelley and Keats,
those muses I loved when life was young. *Come hither,*

I'll plea, *amuse me with your bloody seasons—*
how swiftly they dwindle to mist, such wicked teasing.

I Was the Girl in the Piano Bar

for Avo

He was the man behind the keys
watching me watching him as I leaned in

to listen for my name in his songs.
Gilberto, Sinatra, Scott Joplin. Night after

night, I'd linger in the open-air lounge,
trade winds warm on my bare arms.

Our picnic on a beach, my first taste of tabbouleh
and lamb, the *what if*s of all that blue water.

He was from a different place and time,
and I knew not to follow him home.

*

Tonight a percussionist in a local jazz band
is claiming the stage. So loose,

this stranger in his silk shirt and sandals,
long gray hair tamed into a ponytail.

I feel his brown hands do their work,
spiriting life from wood, bone, gourd—the way

his nimble fingers on a drum are rubbing
the skin of an animal he'll never know.

This Is the Letter I'm Not Writing You

the one about regrets no not that one
the one about love not that one this time
This is the letter I'm not writing you
with its weary list of could-have-beens
should- and would-have-beens if-onlys

but this is not that letter either
This is the letter I'm not writing you
the one that says how much I never mind
the one that wishes we had forget it
This is not that letter

the one I'm not writing you the one
that simply says our last snow was wet
and at the feeders the season's first bluebird
a pair of Baltimore orioles
a yellow-rumped warbler

The Loneliest Whale in the World

after three decades of tracking an elusive whale
from Woods Hole Oceanographic Institute

How to atone for a lone whale calling out
on a fickle note in a cold Pacific sea
        his song unanswered

Calling out on a fickle note
basso profundo a tuba's lowest tone
his song unanswered
        Is he miswired or malformed

Basso profundo
lowest tone on a tuba
his sonic signature oddly pitched
        miswired malformed no one knows

His sonic signature oddly pitched
even scientists say he must be lonely though no one knows
        So here we have it—the whale the sea
the fickle note of a tuba his loneliness

And this—if all life blooms from the sea
and scientists say he must be lonely why can't we
make his keening a primal *ohm*
        song for a new creation

song to be answered in a cold Pacific sea
blooming life and fickle no more
        atonement for a lone and lonely whale

Wrestling with the Legislator Who Denies the Rising of Sea Levels

1.

At first you wished him nightmares,
gut-churning, wake-in-the-middle-of-the-night
nightmares. Or the come-true versions:
his beach house splintered, sandbags lapping up
foam like some hungry whore,

his family uprooted
to the second or third row
where tourists rent by the week
and drink domestic beer.

2.

But what if it's not enough to scorn the one
with heels dug deep in pluff-mud
till there's no more sand to pump,
whose name was blazed by a grandfather
between cottage and surf? You don't wish

his dogs dashed against dunes, do you,
or seagulls adrift without porch rails?
You always loved the gulls
your dogs would chase at water's edge.

3.

You had a grandfather too, remember,
who could spot a dolphin halfway to Spain,
you on a porch swing in the old man's lap,
sun setting on a flat shimmer of salt, he
teaching you each summer about

riptides and undertows and how to pee
in the tidal pools. And in August, how the two
of you would crawl on hands and knees
digging for sharks' teeth—black, prehistoric

endowments you'd pack in a cigar box,
stow deep in the attic forever.

We Walk in Drowned Worms

Void of crimp and wiggle, floating in the churn
of a summer downpour, worms, everywhere worms,

waterlogged. And in the sopping air, oily
vapors rising from the asphalt street like spirits,

our residue let loose. No telling what else
to come forth from deep fantastical portals, unleashed

by the squeeze of saturation. Or what
we might have found if, as kids, we had gone

the way of the dare and somehow dug to China
or some other unsung lullaby—

Indian slums, African babies
made of sticks. Who were we to know

they'd be like us—we,
the puddle-splashers, fortified in L.L.Bean rubber

when gutters turn to flood,
our only muddles those yucky worms

on our new boots,
and all the playgrounds closed.

They've Taken Another One

This time an American aid worker.
Last night while you were sleeping.
Last night while you were not sleeping

but shifting your pillow, trampling
the grasses of a distant dream,
dodging your dark angels.

It could have been your son or daughter,
even a lover. It could have been you. Kneeling
in the night, desert pockmarking your knees,

head stuffed in a feedbag, the wait
for that cold slice of steel through dead air,
your yearning to be swaddled

once more before you sleep.

One Day

from the New York Times—June 17, 2015

After his tango with hot pipes, a steelworker In Cherepovets, Russia, steams stress-free in a mineral bath, a pot of honeyed tea steeping on the stove. In another kitchen, a mother's oven releases a batch of date-filled ring cookies for the Imam's blessing at Ramadan's evening prayer. At a local high school a new student sports a sassy pink updo, his once-blue right of passage transfigured during summer break. And in Spokane a broken narrative holds a woman's heritage hostage, a lie she can neither claim nor resist. Temperatures are searing the west and the Pope has turned politician like a Darwinian finch hardwired for adapta-tion. In a city park, Prospero struts under a canvas of bruised jewels while in the great parade of his tempest all yearn to be goddesses and sprites. Not until later tonight will nine, whose names we don't yet know, be slaughtered in a church basement.

interconnected
shoulder to shoulder we weave
our strange gyrations

Dear Humans

after St. Augustine's treatise on original sin (c.400)

my sin has a forest in it   dark and alive
with misadventures   apples   apples   apples

at night the animals are hungry   snakes
hang on the boughs   blow in the wind chimes

my sin has a song to sing   something about stars
and scabbed knees   and common denominators

my sin cannot be bought   it is aching to free-float
     in bubbles   dandelion seeds

all day my sin sparkles   makes up tales   pretends pretty
mutton and white bread   apple pudding   wafers and wine

it burns my tongue   sweat   fire   stolen pears
     and howls all night at the moon

rips open my secret tributaries   turns tears to floods
washes over us all with blood   red wolf   protozoa   prince

of razzmatazz   then settles into mossy greens
back to the forest   my sin

has convictions   I didn't mean to   she made me do it
and O can my sin dance a jig   calypso   tango

my sin   is your sin   is the sin of snake skin   apple skin
     poison   perfume

Why I Need to Talk about January

because January is a margarita rimmed in salt

because in the scrub brush of the Abacos next to
      the cocktail bar there was a loose chicken
      loose and illusive and I was hungry
          and because I went there in January

because on a different island in a different ocean
      at zero latitude a mangrove grows despite the odds

because a tree like that lives on the edge

because I wanted to live on the edge

because my granddaughter was born in January
      on what would have been my mother's 100th birthday

because my mother may be listening
      and she still wears that flowered dress
      and back-seams in my dreams

because there are plums chattering in the crepe myrtle

because I'm still wanting to talk about the mangrove
      anchored in waterlogged mud
      and the way she spits out her yellow leaves
          to save the world

because I incidentally made her a *she*

because there is salt in those yellow leaves
          and releasing them is a sacrifice—ask
      the shrimp   invertebrates   algae   amphibians

because I know what lies in the roots of that mangrove
      buffer from storm surge
      nectar for rodents and bats

because I'm encrusted in salt

Acknowledgments

Grateful acknowledgment to the editors of the following journals
and anthologies in which these poems, sometimes in an earlier version,
originally appeared:

About Place: "Rack of Lamb," "What If the Mad Farmer Could Sit In on a
New Year's Day Pot Luck during a Global Recession"

Atlanta Review: "While Trying to Let Go of the Dying Sea Lions, I Find
Myself Addressing My Ex-Husband"

Broad River Review: Ron Rash Prize finalist: "Sunset at Six Stories"

Dead Mule School of Southern Literature: "Fish Camp, Indian River,
1956"

Iodine: "Contract," "Best to Leave Creek in the Woods"

Nine Mile Magazine: "Farm to Table, a Blessing," "Salty-Sour-Bitter-
Sweet," "A Mother Dreams of Snow," "Unconformity," "Considering
Castration," "Two Sexagenarians Strolling the Landfill on Green
Turtle Cay," "Linger of Salt and Bone," "Barbeque Pit," "Furnace
Busted, I Think of the Dead," "Why I Need to Talk about January,"
"Trust Fall"

North Carolina Literary Review: James Applewhite Prize finalists:
"In the Mingle of Gods," "Coming in June," "The L Word"

Pembroke Magazine: "Blue in Winter, Blame the Moon"

Southern Women's Review: "Lunch at the Pink Elephant, Old
Girlfriends," "Baking Chicken Pie with My Mother"

Sow's Ear: "'I Went There with My Boyfriend at the Time,' We Overhear
a Woman Say as We Pass Her in the Park," "Pink Clock Radio"

Streetlight Magazine: "We Always Called Him Fletcher," "Wrestling with
the Legislator Who Denies the Rising of Sea Levels"

Tar River Poetry: "Sunflowers"

Wild Goose Poetry Review: "What I Remember Most about God,"
"Urban Book Club Gathers to Discuss *The Grand Design* by
Stephen Hawking on the Week Higgs Boson Is Found," "Killing the
Buddha," "This Is the Letter I'm Not Writing You," "After Attending a
Commemoration of the 1964 Civil Rights Act, I Come Home to Find
a Bat in My Bedroom"

Anthologized Poems:

Intimacy, Jacar Press Anthology: "March on Washington, 50th
Anniversary"

Kakalak: 2013: "Naming the Snake"; 2014: "Cows Waiting in an Irish Field"; 2015: "Fishing in White Lace"; 2017: "Male Olive Ridley Sea Turtle Hanging Dead," "Woman with Broken Shell"

Southern Poetry Anthology, North Carolina: "A Potter Tries to Explain Why the Day of a Kiln Opening Is His Most Difficult"

Streetlight 2016, Annual Magazine Collection: "We Always Called Him Fletcher," "Wrestling with the Legislator Who Denies the Rising of Sea Levels"

What Matters, Jacar Press: "Last Meal, Death Row"

"Tabula Rasa" first appeared in a chapbook, *The Gravity of Color,* published by Main Street Rag.

"Homeless" first appeared under the title "Hands" in *Waiting for Soup,* published by Main Street Rag, edited by Barbara Conrad.

"Sunset at Six Stories" was a Ron Rash Prize published finalist for *Broad River Review,* 2015.

"In the Mingle of Gods," "Coming in June" and "The L Word" were published finalists for *North Carolina Literary Review*'s 2015 James Applewhite Prize.

"I Was the Girl in the Piano Bar" was a designated semifinalist for the 2016 James Applewhite Prize, *North Carolina Literary Review.*

I am deeply grateful to my poetry groups and writing community for all they have done to make this book a reality, for their time, their talent and their friendship. For my long-vibrant Wednesday group: Rebecca McClanahan, Gail Peck, Diana Pinckney, Barbara Presnell, Dede Wilson; for those who gather around Dannye's table on Fridays: Eleanor Brawley, Bobbie Campbell, Jennifer Hubbard, Jerry Jernigan, Mary Kratt, Janet Miller, Charles Murray, Tootsie O'Hara, Dannye Romine Powell, Peg Robarchek, Beth Swann and Lisa Zerkle; for my first teacher who got me started, Irene Honeycutt, and to both Irene and Joseph Bathanti for taking the time and effort to read and comment on this book; for mentors who have kept me going, especially Tony Abbot, and for the spirit muses who continue to guide me, Susan Myers and Henry Berne. And a special shout-out to my FutureCycle editor, Diane Kistner, for her extraordinary guidance and patient support in bringing this book to life.

About FutureCycle Press

FutureCycle Press is dedicated to publishing lasting English-language poetry books, chapbooks, and anthologies in both print-on-demand and Kindle ebook formats. Founded in 2007 by long-time independent editor/publishers and partners Diane Kistner and Robert S. King, the press incorporated as a nonprofit in 2012. A number of our editors are distinguished poets and writers in their own right, and we have been actively involved in the small press movement going back to the early seventies.

The FutureCycle Poetry Book Prize and honorarium is awarded annually for the best full-length volume of poetry we publish in a calendar year. Introduced in 2013, our Good Works projects are anthologies devoted to issues of universal significance, with all proceeds donated to a related worthy cause. Our Selected Poems series highlights contemporary poets with a substantial body of work to their credit; with this series we strive to resurrect work that has had limited distribution and is now out of print.

We are dedicated to giving all of the authors we publish the care their work deserves, making our catalog of titles the most diverse and distinguished it can be, and paying forward any earnings to fund more great books.

We've learned a few things about independent publishing over the years. We've also evolved a unique, resilient publishing model that allows us to focus mainly on vetting and preserving for posterity poetry collections of exceptional quality without becoming overwhelmed with bookkeeping and mailing, fundraising activities, or taxing editorial and production "bubbles." To find out more about what we are doing, come see us at www.futurecycle.org.

The FutureCycle Poetry Book Prize

All full-length volumes of poetry published by FutureCycle Press in a given calendar year are considered for the annual FutureCycle Poetry Book Prize. This allows us to consider each submission on its own merits, outside of the context of a contest. Too, the judges see the finished book, which will have benefitted from the beautiful book design and strong editorial gloss we are famous for.

The book ranked the best in judging is announced as the prize-winner in the subsequent year. There is no fixed monetary award; instead, the winning poet receives an honorarium of 20% of the total net royalties from all poetry books and chapbooks the press sold online in the year the winning book was published. The winner is also accorded the honor of being on the panel of judges for the next year's competition; all judges receive copies of all contending books to keep for their personal library.

www.ingramcontent.com/pod-product-compliance
Lightning Source LLC
Chambersburg PA
CBHW070007100426
42741CB00012B/3136